Contents

What is Sikhism?

Guru Nanak started the Sikh religion in the 1400s in Punjab, in what is now part of Pakistan and north-west India. For Sikhs, the word 'Guru' means a spiritual guide who teaches God's message. Sikhs use the word 'Guru' only for Guru Nanak, his nine successors and the Sikh holy book, the Guru Granth Sahib.

What do Sikhs believe?

Sikhs believe in one God. There are many names for God but the one most commonly used is Waheguru. The Gurus taught that God is neither male nor female, and is without any image or form. God is not born and does not die and is present everywhere in the universe that he has created.

◄ The Sri Harimander Sahib (The Golden Temple) in Amritsar, India which stands in the middle of an artificial lake. Sikhs from all over the world come to visit The Golden Temple.

▲ This is Sis Ganj, the place where Guru Tegh Bahadur was beheaded. Now there is a Sikh place of worship built on the site.

Respect for all

Sikhs think that all religions are just different paths to God and that no single religion is the only true one. Sikhism teaches people to respect other people's beliefs and to protect the right of others to follow their religion. Sikhs learn about the ninth Guru, called Tegh Bahadur, who was beheaded for defending the right of Hindus to practise their religion.

Equality

Sikhs believe that God made all people equal. The Guru wrote:
'From the Divine Light the whole creation sprang. Why then should we divide human creatures Into high and low?
The Lord the maker has moulded one mass of clay Into diverse shapes.'
He is saying that God created all human beings out of the same material. People may all be different but they are all equal.

Sikhism worldwide

Today, there are about 14 million Sikhs. Most still live in Punjab, but there are also large Sikh communities in other places, such as Britain and North America. Wherever they live, Sikh men wear a turban as a symbol of their faith.

5

The first Guru

Guru Nanak was born into a Hindu family in 1469, in Punjab. At his birth, it was predicted that he would praise God and teach others to praise him, too. When he grew up, Nanak worked as a cattle herder and then as an accountant. Always ready to help the needy, he spent most of his wages on feeding poor people.

God's message

One morning, when Nanak was 30 years old, he went to bathe in the river. He disappeared and people thought that he had drowned. Three days later, he reappeared and remained silent for a whole day. Then he uttered the words, "There is neither a Hindu nor a Muslim, only God's path and I shall follow God's path." He meant that all human beings are equal in God's eyes. God is not interested in the labels Hindu, Muslim, Jew, Christian or Sikh. It is the behaviour and good actions of people that are important.

◄ This is a picture of Guru Nanak sitting with his two companions: Bala, a Hindu and Mardana, a Muslim.

Equality of women

During Guru Nanak's time, women were treated very badly and were considered to be lower in status than men. But Guru Nanak taught: 'How can we call women bad, when great people are born from them?' A Sikh girl does not take her father's name or, later on, her husband's. She is an individual in her own right.

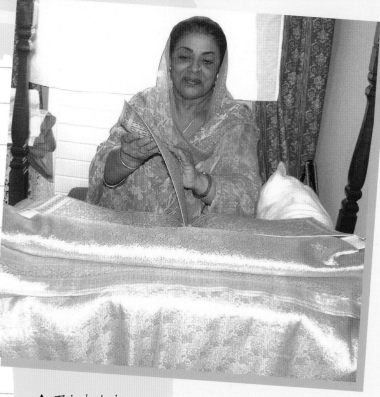

▲ This lady is reading the Guru Granth Sahib. Sikh women perform ceremonies and take services along with men.

◄ This picture shows Guru Nanak preaching in the court of Emperor Babar.

Spreading the word

Guru Nanak took four long journeys to spread his message about God's path and the way to lead a truthful life. He taught that all human beings, black or white, rich or poor, high or low, men or women are equal before God. Guru Nanak believed that it was important to teach by example. He said, 'Truth is high, but higher is truthful living.'

Religion at war

Nanak talked to people about God and their beliefs. He learnt about Hinduism and Islam, the major religions in India. He was unhappy to see Hindus and Muslims fighting, each one claiming that their religion was the better.

7

The other nine Gurus

Guru Nanak chose Guru Angad Dev to be the next Guru after his own death, and each Guru after that chose the one who would follow them. Sikhs think of the Gurus' spirits as being like candles, each one lit from the one before. There were ten human Gurus in all. They led the Sikhs as the community grew and developed. The tenth Guru gave Guruship to the Guru Granth Sahib, a holy book. He asked the Sikh people to follow the teachings written in the Guru Granth Sahib.

Guru Angad Dev, the second Guru

All the Gurus wrote in Punjabi, the language of ordinary people, so that men and women of every class could understand their writings. Guru Angad Dev simplified the lettering, called Gurmurkhi, used for writing Punjabi, to make it as clear as possible to read.

Guru Arjan Dev, the fifth Guru

Guru Arjan completed the building of the Golden Temple (see page 27). He collected together the writings of the previous four Gurus, his own writings and those of many Hindu and Muslim saints, to form the Sikh holy book, the Guru Granth Sahib.

Guru Hargobind, the sixth Guru

Guru Hargobind became Guru after his father was killed for refusing to become a Muslim. He realized the need for people to defend themselves from their rulers. He wore two swords, one as a symbol of God's Truth and the other to remind Sikhs of the importance of their worldly power to defend the weak.

▼ The ten Gurus and the Guru Granth Sahib.

The 52 princes

Guru Hargobind was imprisoned by the emperor on a false charge of treason. The emperor freed him but the Guru refused to leave the prison until 52 innocent Hindu princes were also released. The emperor agreed to free only those princes who could pass through the jail's narrow exit, while holding onto the Guru's cloak. The Guru's Sikhs made him a cloak with 52 tassels of different lengths. Then all the princes walked free, each one holding onto a tassel!

9

The Sikhs' holy book

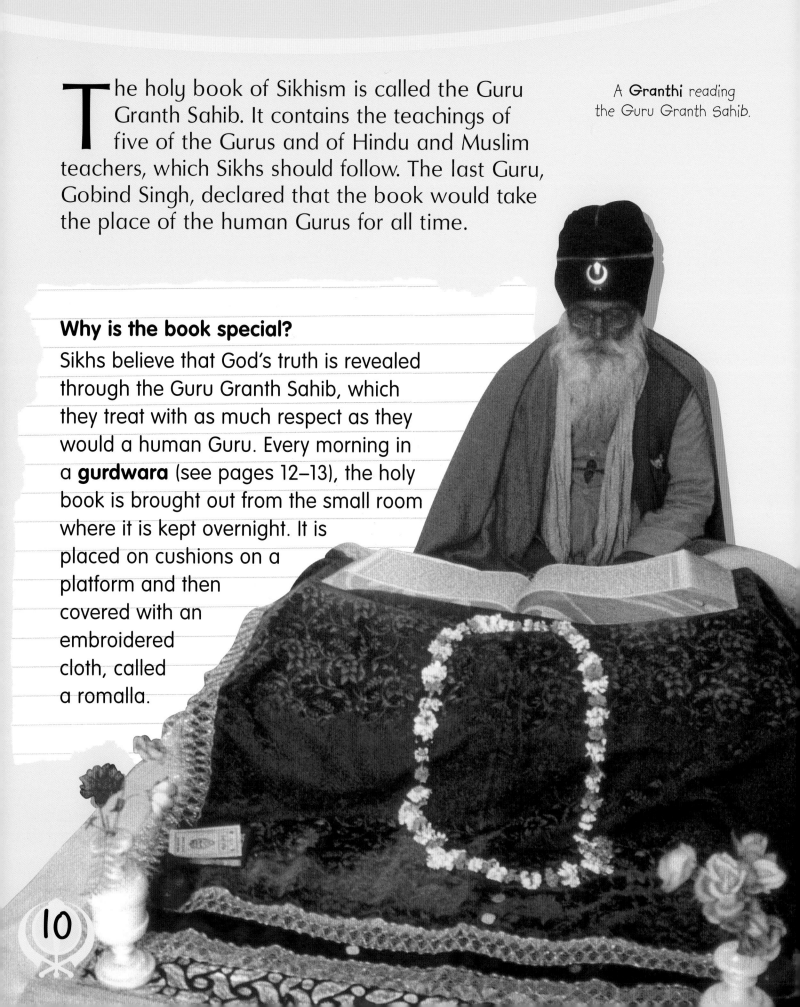

The holy book of Sikhism is called the Guru Granth Sahib. It contains the teachings of five of the Gurus and of Hindu and Muslim teachers, which Sikhs should follow. The last Guru, Gobind Singh, declared that the book would take the place of the human Gurus for all time.

A **Granthi** reading the Guru Granth Sahib.

Why is the book special?

Sikhs believe that God's truth is revealed through the Guru Granth Sahib, which they treat with as much respect as they would a human Guru. Every morning in a **gurdwara** (see pages 12–13), the holy book is brought out from the small room where it is kept overnight. It is placed on cushions on a platform and then covered with an embroidered cloth, called a romalla.

What's in it?

Inside the Guru Granth Sahib are hymns that praise God, tell us what he is like and how to lead a good life. They are written mainly in the Punjabi language. Each copy of the book has 1,430 pages and each hymn is found on the same page in every copy.

▲ A Granthi reading the Guru Granth Sahib in the famous Harimandar Sahib (Golden Temple).

At home

Some Sikhs keep a copy of the Guru Granth Sahib at home, in a separate room which can be called the gurdwara (see page 12). All Sikhs also keep a book containing hymns copied from the Guru Granth Sahib. Many people memorize the hymns and recite them daily. They treat the hymn book with respect.

Make a Punjabi symbol

You will need:
thin white card • pencil • scissors • paints, pens or crayons • sequins or glitter.

1 Use a pencil to draw the two parts of the symbol onto the card. Take care to copy the symbol as accurately as you can.

2 Carefully cut around the two pieces. Use pens, crayons or paints to colour in the symbol. Then decorate it with glitter or sequins.

3 Stick the symbol to a window or hang it up as a mobile. The symbol means 'There is only one God' in the Punjabi language.

11

Places of worship

A Sikh place of worship is called a gurdwara, which means 'the door of the Guru'. Many gurdwaras in India are built in memory of events in the Gurus' lives. The most famous gurdwara of all is the Harimandir Sahib, or Golden Temple (see page 27). Wherever the Guru Granth Sahib (see pages 10–11) is kept is called a gurdwara, even if this is a room in an ordinary house.

Inside the gurdwara

A gurdwara has a prayer hall and a dining hall, a room in which to keep the Guru Granth Sahib, a library and a classroom where the Punjabi language and music are taught. Anyone may read from the Guru Granth Sahib, but often it is read by a Granthi, a person who leads the prayers. Musicians called **ragis** sing hymns and play the tabla (drums) and harmonium.

◄ When people enter the prayer hall in a gurdwara, they bow to the Guru Granth Sahib as a mark of respect.

▲ After the prayers, the congregation eat together. This is to show that all human beings belong to one family of God.

The Sikh worship

During the act of worship, people sit on the floor, as a sign that all are equal.

The Granthi sits behind the Guru Granth Sahib waving a **chauri** (fan) over it in the same way that a fan would have been waved over a prince in India. At the end of the service, a sweet food called **karah prasad** is shared out. People make token offerings of cash or food for the meal that is served afterwards.

The dining hall

Everyone eats the free **langar** (meal) in the dining hall after the service. Before the Gurus existed, people who were from the lower class were not allowed to eat with those from the higher class. The Gurus taught that all people are God's children and should eat together like one family. The food is always vegetarian so that those who do not eat meat can join in. It is made and served by volunteers. Sikhs are taught to give their time, money and any skills they have freely to others.

Family celebrations

Family life is important to Sikhs and special events are marked by ceremonies to seek God's blessing. These occasions always take place in the presence of the Guru Granth Sahib to show the importance of the Sikh teachings in everything a Sikh does, during good or difficult times. Hymns are sung, prayers are said and food is provided for the guests.

◄ Parents of the bride put garlands on the couple to congratulate them after the wedding service.

Marriage

Partners are introduced to one another by their families, but the couple themselves decide whether to marry. The bride wears pink or red (the colours of happiness) and the bridegroom wears a red or pink turban and a special scarf, called a pala. The bride's father places one end of the pala in the bride's hand as a symbol that they are joined as husband and wife. The Guru Granth Sahib is opened and the marriage hymn is read. After each of the four verses, the couple walk slowly around the Guru Granth Sahib, with the groom leading.

Death

Sikhs believe that death is not the end. When a person dies, the soul moves on to another body and keeps moving on until it is reunited with God. The family you are born into is decided according to karma (good or bad actions in the previous life), but you can come closer to God by leading a good life. After cremation, the dead person's ashes are scattered on water either in a river or the sea.

The naming ceremony

When a baby is born, the family goes to the gurdwara, where the Guru Granth Sahib is opened at random. The family chooses a name for the baby that begins with the first letter of that day's reading. Boys also take the surname Singh (lion), while girls take Kaur (princess).

Patka tying

Until a boy is old enough to wear a turban (normally at secondary school), he covers his uncut hair with a patka. This is a square piece of material with a string attached at each corner. First, his hair is tied into a top knot, then the patka is put in place and finally the corner strings are used to secure the patka. A boy also might wear a roomal, which is a small handkerchief tied over the top knot.

15

Festivals

Sikh festivals celebrate the birth, death or another event in the life of one of the Gurus. There are street processions and the whole of the Guru Granth Sahib is read aloud, which takes two days, starting before the main celebration. Langar (see page 13) is served throughout the three-day festival.

Important birthdays

The birthdays of Guru Nanak, the founder of Sikhism, and Guru Gobind Singh, the last human Guru, are important festivals. Gurdwaras, shops and houses are lit up with candles. Children are given new clothes. During street processions, the Guru Granth Sahib is carried on a decorated float. Bands of children play music and there are Sikh martial arts displays.

Divali

Divali means 'festival of lights'. On Divali day, Sikhs light lamps to celebrate Guru Hargobind's release from prison (see page 9). In Amritsar, India, Sikhs illuminate the whole of the Golden Temple and celebrate with wonderful firework displays.

▲ In this painting, Guru Hargobind is shown coming out of prison followed by the 52 Hindu princes holding the tassels on his cloak (see page 9).

Flag ceremony

Vaisakhi is a new year festival that celebrates the day when Sikhism was born. On this day at the gurdwara, the **Nishan Sahib** (the sikh flag featuring the **khanda**) is replaced with a new cloth and the flagpole is cleaned.

▶ A new cloth is being fixed to the cleaned flagpole to celebrate Vaisakhi.

Make a khanda stencil

You will need: thick card • pencil and ruler • craft knife • cutting board • masking tape • fabric or paper • sponge or roller • paint

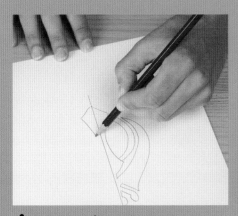

1 Draw a line down the middle of the card and copy half the Khanda symbol. Draw the other half so they are symmetrical.

2 Ask an adult to cut around the lines with a craft knife. Tape the edges of the stencil you have made to fabric or paper.

3 Dab paint through the stencil with a sponge or roller. Remove the stencil and let the print dry.

How the Khalsa was created

One April day, in 1699, Guru Gobind Singh, the tenth Sikh Guru, tested his Sikhs to see if they were brave enough to stand up for their beliefs.

The Guru said, "I need a Sikh, who is willing to sacrifice his life for God and the Guru." One man in the crowd got up and was led into the Guru's tent. The Guru came out of the tent with a blood-soaked sword and asked for another volunteer. Another Sikh came forward to give his life. After the fifth Sikh had disappeared inside the tent, the crowd nervously waited for the Guru to come out.

They gasped when they saw the Guru walk out of the tent with all five of the Sikhs following behind him. They all had their hair tied up under their turbans and were now dressed in fine clothes.

The Guru explained that he had been testing his Sikhs and said, "The five Sikhs have shown courage and are my beloved ones." The Five Beloved ones are known as the **Panja piare**.

The Guru poured water into an iron bowl and stirred it with a sword called a **khanda**, while reciting five prayers. The Guru's wife added some sugar and the Guru said, "You have made the ceremony complete. A resolve of steel should be combined with a sweetness of temperament." The Guru gave the drink, called **amrit**, to the five Sikhs. Once they had drunk the amrit, they became the first five members of the Khalsa, the holy order of Sikhs. He called for Khalsa Sikhs to wear certain clothes, called the Five Ks, from then on to show their Sikh identity. No longer could Sikhs hide in the crowd, even in difficult times. The Guru asked them to take new names. He asked Khalsa Sikh men to take the name Singh, which means 'lion', to remind them of the need for courage. To all Khalsa Sikh women, the Guru gave the name Kaur, which means 'princess', so that they would never forget their dignity and total equality with men.

Joining the Sikh community

Anyone can join the Khalsa, the community of Sikhs willing to give their lives for their faith. There is no minimum age laid down for joining. However, people are advised to join when they fully understand its importance and can keep the vows they take. These include treating everyone as equal, defending the weak and respecting people of other religions.

The ceremony

People joining the community receive a holy liquid called amrit. Clean water and sugar crystals are put in a steel bowl. A Sikh leader stirs the water with the khanda (the double-edged sword), while reciting five special prayers. Those taking amrit, receive it in cupped hands and drink it five times. The amrit is also sprinkled five times over their eyes and hair. The people joining the community are also given some duties, such as reciting special prayers every day to remind them to look after people who are less fortunate than themselves.

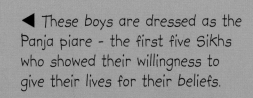
◀ These boys are dressed as the Panja piare - the first five Sikhs who showed their willingness to give their lives for their beliefs.

The Five Ks

People joining the Khalsa are given five symbols to wear. These are known as the Five Ks, as each one begins with a 'k'.

Kes – uncut hair. Men tie their hair up and cover it with a turban. Women keep their hair loose, plaited or tied in a bun at the back of the neck.

▲ A Sikh wearing a Kara.

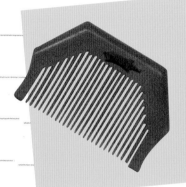

Kanga – a comb. A small wooden comb is worn in the hair to keep the hair neat. It also represents general cleanliness.

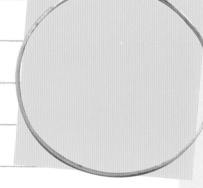

Kara – a steel or iron bangle. This is not worn as a piece of jewellery but to bind Sikhs to God and remind them of their duty to do the right thing.

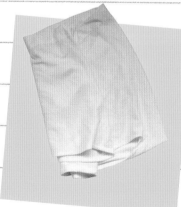

Kach – cotton underwear. This reminds Sikhs of purity and self-control.

Kirpan – a sword. This is a symbol of God's supreme power and also reminds Sikhs of their duty to defend the weak.

Around the world

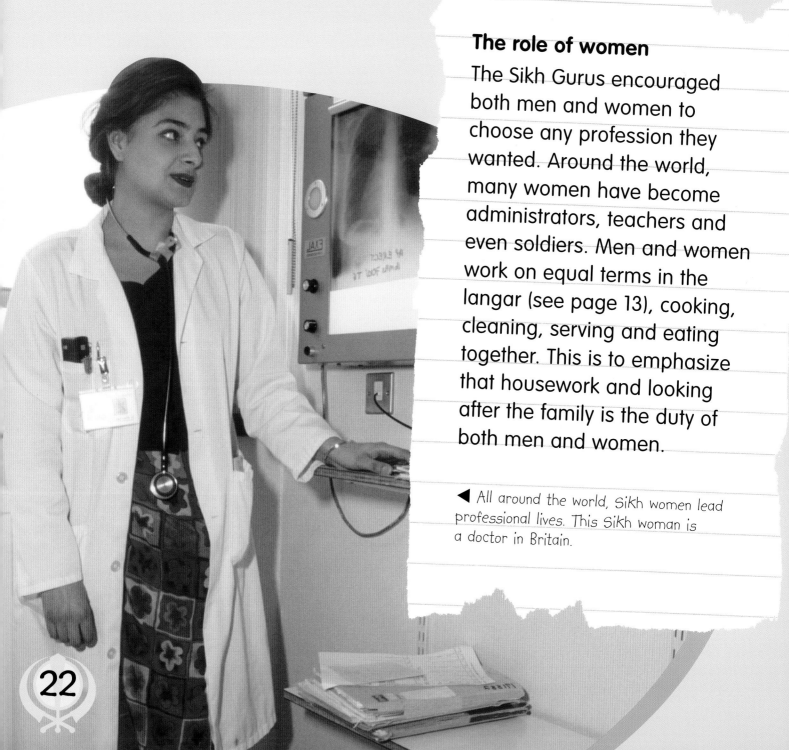

From its origins in Punjab, in India, Sikhism has spread all over the world, to the USA, Canada, Britain, Australia, Singapore, Malaysia and many other countries. About 400,000 Sikhs live in Britain, the largest number living anywhere outside India. One third of the Sikh population of Britain lives in Greater London.

The role of women

The Sikh Gurus encouraged both men and women to choose any profession they wanted. Around the world, many women have become administrators, teachers and even soldiers. Men and women work on equal terms in the langar (see page 13), cooking, cleaning, serving and eating together. This is to emphasize that housework and looking after the family is the duty of both men and women.

◀ All around the world, Sikh women lead professional lives. This Sikh woman is a doctor in Britain.

► Sikh children singing shabads (hymns from the Guru Granth Sahib) during a service in the gurdwara.

The three golden rules

Wherever they live, Sikhs believe in the 'three golden rules':

To remember God by reflecting on his qualities as described in the Guru Granth Sahib. Remembering God leads people to live good lives and to work for the benefit of society.

To earn enough, by means of hard work, to look after themselves and their families. However, they should not let money dominate their lives.

To share money, time or skills to help others who have less. This is known as sewa (voluntary work). Many gurdwaras have opened hospitals and schools, offering free beds and food. The people who use these facilities also take part in sewa by cleaning or helping in the langar.

The Punjabi language

Sikhs who live outside India may find it hard to understand religious texts written in the Punjabi language and the Punjabi prayers. So most gurdwaras hold Punjabi language classes, and also conferences and camps to teach the Sikh way of life.

Sikh customs

Wherever they may live in the world, there are certain customs that Sikhs follow. For example, an extended family, where different generations of the same family live together, is still common. The Sikh religion teaches that different age groups should respect and take care of each other.

Dress code

There are no hard and fast rules about what Sikh men and women should wear, except that Sikh men have to wear a turban. The turban is tied around the head so that it fits the person's head comfortably. There is no significance in the colour of the turban. Most Sikhs match the turban to their shirt, tie or suit, but some wear white or black all the time. Young Sikh boys mostly wear a patka (see page 15).

◄ A gathering of an extended Sikh family at the home of their grandparents.

Food

Sikhs can eat anything, except meat from an animal that has been killed by **ritual**. Everyone eats flat bread with vegetable curry, dal (lentils) and yoghurt. Samosas (pastries filled with potatoes and peas) and pakoras (vegetables fried in chickpea batter) are popular snacks. At the end of every Sikh worship in the gurdwara, the 'holy sweet' karah prasad is served.

▶ The type of food normally eaten at a gurdwara.

Sikh greeting

When a Sikh meets another Sikh, they greet each other with the phrase 'Sat Siri Akal.' This means 'Immortal God is the Truth' and reminds Sikhs about the importance of truth in all circumstances.

Make some holy sweets

You will need: 200ml water • saucepan • 80g sugar • jug • 90g butter • 100g semolina

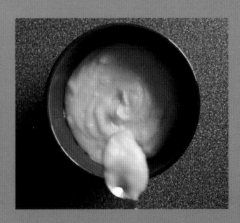

1 Boil 200ml of water in a saucepan. Add the sugar and wait until it has dissolved in the boiling water. Pour the mixture into a jug and leave it to one side.

2 Melt the butter in the saucepan, then add the semolina. Stir over a moderate heat until it is golden brown. Add the sugared water and stir until the mixture has thickened.

3 Leave it to cool. Then share the karah prasad with your friends. You can eat it with a spoon, or with your fingers – like in the gurdwara – if your hands are clean!

25

Art and crafts

In India, most Sikhs are farmers who work hard with little spare time, so most Sikh art and crafts take place at home. Sikh folk music, called **bhangra**, is world famous, as is the architecture of Harimandir Sahib (the Golden Temple) in Amritsar.

Music

Music is an important part of worship in the gurdwara. Each hymn in the Guru Granth Sahib has its own traditional tune. Bhangra music is popular in Sikh homes. Bhangra dancing is energetic with a fast beat. The dance can be done by any number of people, accompanied by a big drum. The success of the dance depends on the quality of the drummer.

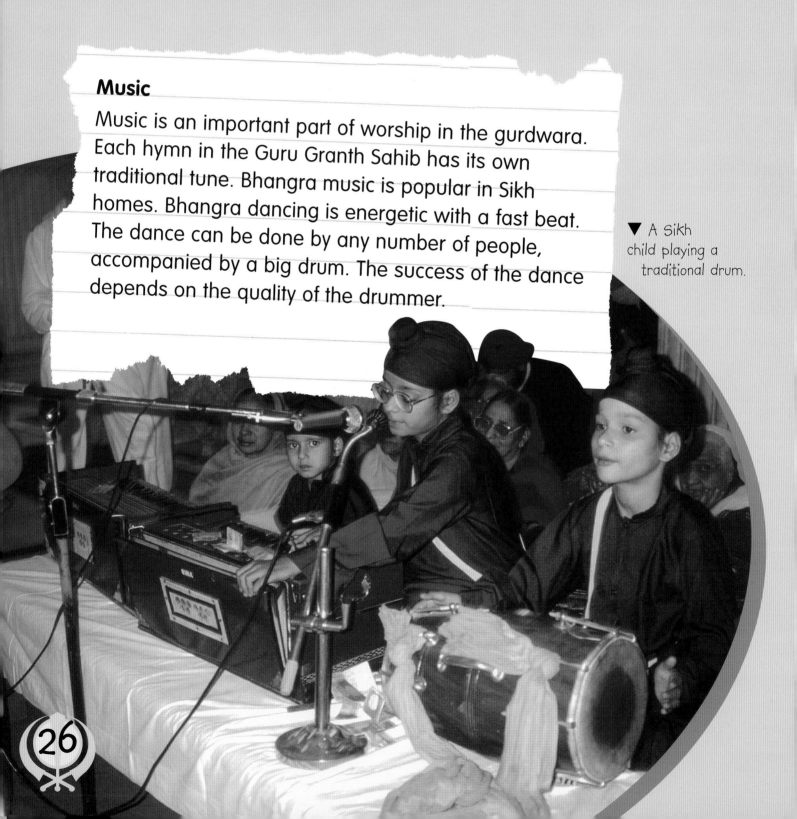

▼ A Sikh child playing a traditional drum.

Embroidery

The finest of all Sikh arts is embroidery, and it is taught from mother to daughter. Fabrics are woven with intricate geometric designs. In the past, girls made embroidered wall hangings to take to their in-laws' houses as marriage gifts.

▲ The base colour of the embroidery is always dark red. Colourful, complicated, geometric designs stand out against this strong background.

Martial art

Gatka is a Sikh martial art of self-defence, like karate, judo and kung fu. It is based on rapid movements of the feet and hands while holding a strong stick or a sword, and is similar to fencing. Gatka groups perform in gurdwaras and in street processions on festival days. Both men and women take part in gatka.

▶ Sikhs bathing in the lake at the Harimandir Sahib (Golden Temple), India.

Architecture

Sikh architecture combines the best features of Hindu and Muslim design. The Harimandir Sahib is a gurdwara built in the middle of an artificial lake, in which visitors often bathe. The dome and the top half of the outside walls are covered with gold plate. Inside, the walls are decorated with a rare blend of brass and copper, inlaid with beautiful, coloured precious stones.

27

Activity

Make a model of the Golden Temple

A marble walkway leads from the edge of the lake and runs around the outside of the Golden Temple. It has double doors on all four sides, making it easy for all to come and pray together.

You will need:

A small cardboard box • thin card • hemispherical yoghurt pot • pencil and ruler • scissors • craft knife • glue • white paper • gold paper or gold paint or spray paint

• red, blue and green paper • sequins • toothpick • scrap of yellow paper • mirror larger than your box (or silver foil and cardboard)

1 Draw four double doors, one door in the centre of each side of the box. Draw a line down the middle of each door and cut them with a craft knife so that they open, as shown.

2 Use a ruler and pencil to draw a horizontal line all the way around middle of the box, above the double doors, to divide it into two halves.

3 Measure and cut a long strip of thin card about 10cm wide, that fits around the box with a 2cm overlap. Cut curved shapes out of one long edge to form the arches of the parapet.

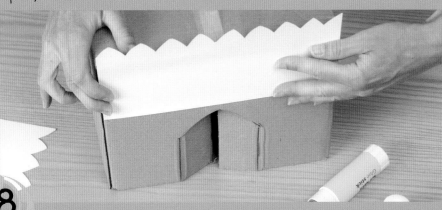

4 Wrap the card around the box, so that the arches stick up above the top of the box. Glue the card in place.

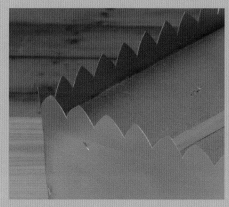

5 Paint or spray the roof and the top half of the box with gold paint or spray paint (with adult help) or cover it with gold paper.

6 Paint the yoghurt pot gold. Use masking tape to stick it to the top of the box for the dome, making sure it sits in the middle.

7 Cover the lower part of the building with white paper. Use a ruler and pen to draw thin black lines to look like rectangular tiles.

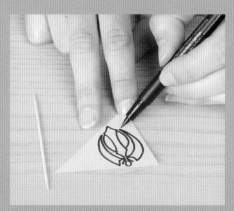

8 Put your model in the middle of a mirror or a piece of cardboard covered in foil. Cut white paper squares and glue them down to look like a tiled, marble walkway.

9 Cut a small yellow triangle of paper for the flag and draw a khanda symbol on it. Attach the flag to one end of the toothpick and stick it on the dome.

Add more decoration if you wish. Cut patterns from red, green and blue paper to decorate the tiles. Glue on sequins to look like precious jewels.

Glossary

Amrit A sweet drink made by stirring sugar crystals into water with a double-edged sword, while certain passages from the scriptures are recited. Amrit means nectar.

Bhangra A type of music and dancing, originally from the Punjab, which is now popular around the world.

Chauri A fan made of yak hair or nylon. This is waved over the holy book, the Guru Granth Sahib, to show respect for the scriptures.

Granthi Someone who reads the Guru Granth Sahib outloud, leads prayers and conducts ceremonies.

Gurdwara A place where the holy book, the Guru Granth Sahib, is kept. It also means a place of worship.

Khanda A double-edged sword used in the amrit ceremony. It is pictured on the Sikh flag, the Nishan Sahib.

Karah prasad Sweet pudding made from butter, flour, sugar and water. Karah prasad is shared at the end of Sikh gatherings to show equality.

Langar The name for the meal eaten during a service and also for the free food provided by the gurdwara.

Nishan Sahib The Sikh flag. It is saffron-coloured and triangular, with a picture of the khanda in the centre.

Panja piare The name for the first five members of the Khalsa, the holy order of Sikhs.

Ragis Sikh musicians who lead and sing shabads (hymns) from the holy book, the Guru Granth Sahib.

Ritual A ceremonial act. Some cultures kill animals in a certain way to please their God. Sikhs do not believe in doing this.

Index

Notes for parents and teachers

This book aims to give an introduction to Sikhism. It does not cover all aspect of the religion but gives a start to readers to take their own initiative to study the religion further. It also links closely to the Non Statutory Framework for Religious Education, especially to the following schemes of work, which feature in most of the local Agreed Syllabuses.

- What does it mean to belong?
- Celebrations
- Visiting a place of worship
- Importance of praying and eating together
- What do signs and symbols mean in religion?
- Importance of the 5Ks for Sikhs
- Why do Sikhs pray at home and the gurdwara?
- Why do Sikhs celebrate Vaisakhi?
- Importance of Guru Granth Sahib for Sikhs

Visiting a Gurdwara

The best way to learn about Sikhism is to visit a gurdwara. There you will see the basic Sikh principle of 'one God and equality for all humans' being implemented. All gurdwaras welcome visitors. Anyone who wishes to pray to one God can join in the prayers and eat the langar, a free community meal, at the end. All visitors are required to observe the traditions. For example, everyone should cover their heads and take off their shoes before entering the gurdwara. If you forget to take a head covering, gurdwaras usually provide one. Tobacco and alcohol are not allowed in the gurdwara precincts. If you want, you can take photos inside the gurdwara, but it is always polite to ask first.

To make the best use of your visit, write a list of things to see and questions to ask beforehand.

More books to read

Keystones: Sikh Gurdwara
Kanwaljit Kaur-Singh, A&C Black 2000

My Life, My Religion: Sikh Granthi
Kanwaljit Kaur-Singh, Franklin Watts 2001

Where We Worship: Sikh Gurdwara
Kanwaljit Kaur-Singh, Franklin Watts 2005

Start-Up Religion: Visiting a Gurdwara
Kanwaljit Kaur-Singh and Ruth Nason, Evans 2005

Sikhism For Today
Kanwaljit Kaur-Singh, Oxford University Press 2004

Stories About Sikh Tradition
Kanwaljit Kaur-Singh, Hemkunt Press 2006

Useful websites

www.nsouk.co.uk
A useful site for general information on Sikhism

www.allaboutsikhs.com
Gives detailed information on different aspects of Sikhism

www.sikhnet.com
For Sikh news